AMULET

SAINT JULIAN PRESS

POETRY

Praise for AMULET

It's true, as Stephanie Kartalopoulos writes, "[t]here is too much / in this world already." But the poet turns toward it all with her imaginative, insightful voice, her edgy desire, and her unflinching eye, spinning our skeletons into the most poetic amber. These poems are "imperishable," amulets for the world, and the light that shines through is alive, warm, stunning.

—Amy Newman, author of *Dear Editor*
and *On This Day in Poetry History*

Even as Kartalopoulos declares that "there is too much in the world already" and "everything is breaking," these richly polysemous poems invite us to investigate the places where dislocation and decay are barely distinguishable from intimations of the new. With oblique, associational logic, under varied constellations and in mutating weathers, she ponders the algorithmic interweavings of love, family, and soul-making in American and Greece as she labors to "account for...tectonic shift...deformational history" and create "a way to say the being of your hour."

—Claire Bateman,
author of *Scape* and *Locals: A Collection of Prose Poems*

Stephanie Kartalopoulos's *Amulet* is a breathtakingly beautiful book that embodies negative capability, though her poetics is less Keatsian than Dickinsonian definition and redefinition. Frequently, the poems define their space by delineating what is not, defying expectations and received ideas: "This is not lightning, /this is not the razor-fast. Instead, a slow-dreaming machine pushing me / through my mad scene, bringing my soprano-pitch / past its breathless height." Perhaps this kind of causation—if this, then that—a logic of illogic that takes us into utterly surprising places has to do with Kartalopoulos's being Greek-American. Her diasporic voice portrays a familiar third cultural phenomenon—feeling at home and not at home in a unique and innovative way. She asks "What if x" and opens up for us vast and mysterious vistas: "Then maybe its own equation: luminous and blinking: / blanketing the mapped thought of what could be possible."

—Aliki Barnstone, author of *Dwelling* and *Bright Body*

AMULET

Poems

By

Stephanie Kartalopoulos

SAINT JULIAN PRESS
HOUSTON

Published by
SAINT JULIAN PRESS, Inc.
2053 Cortlandt, Suite 200
Houston, Texas 77008

www.saintjulianpress.com

ISBN-13: 978-0-9986404-7-1
ISBN: 0-9986404-7-6
Library of Congress Control Number: 2018935912

Cover Art: *POOL* by Kate McCammon
Author Photo: Thomas Schofield © 2018

for my grandmother,
and for my grandfather.

CONTENTS

This is the force of faith. Nobody gets
what they want. Never again are you the same. The longing
is to be pure. What you get is to be changed.

—Jorie Graham, "Prayer"

AMULET

INSIDE A DARK ROOM

Bruised magnolias, damaged street signs,
a fractured spinal cord. There is too much
in this world already. In a pile,

a picture of one foggy day on the pier
where I hung my shoes from a post and walked
barefoot. Night, unflappable and full of sorrow.

Lamps stuttered into their oily glow.
A mother and her daughter argued over where
to put their furniture, the worth of an isosceles

triangle, what the girl would study in school.
I walked past and hoped that no fault line
would slip between them. Termites

eat their way through my attic.
Ghost limbs pace the length of this room.
There is too much in this world already.

SLOW FAIL

A monocle, some opera gloves:
                                        the down-turn starts
with these things hidden in a dark spot. Like a dried-flower corsage.
Or a Swiss dancer's costume. Kept safe from a watchful eye,

or high noon, the nosy landlord. And then the careful cleaning
of the fingertips, a play against the desire to jump
from spot to spot, a quiet formality over the smallest space

there has ever been to wash.
                                        Somewhere there's the thought
that maybe I am falling out of fashion, a whining
and frailing Cleopatra, a stretch of kohl across the wrong skin,

and not even the lightest thought that this is wrong.
This is not lightning,
                                        this is not the razor-fast.
Instead, a slow-dreaming machine pushing me

through my mad scene, bringing my soprano-pitch
past its breathless height. Eventually a puckered mouth,
a dry tongue,
                                a salty taste for even the sweetest moment.

TO MARY BRASS

It is dim in the beginning, like old lightning.
And then a quiet that deepens into the spellbind
of nerve endings, the thousands of them dangling

and waiting for something to catch and stick.
This is what it is to run out of time.
You are somewhere in my periphery,

like the dogwood trees leaning in their pre-
bloom wind. You are counting quarters
to make sure there are enough to do the washing,

pay the milkman, buy a soda with crushed ice
from the corner store. You are taped along the edges
of an old picture board, standing under a tree

bent hard in an electrical storm, clearing a space
for an iris bed, worried and swollen and hovering
over an open grave. And without a flashing thought,

you are telling me the same thing over and over again:
this is what it is to be in deference to something else.
This is what it is to think you could ever be limitless.

TO REACH METEORA

You need to drive
past tomato fields,

villages, and crumbling churches.
The roads shimmy around mountains

that will not repeat stories
about their people.

All the priests have gone.
Families like mine left for the cities

long ago, leaving their widowed
yiayias to sit by the dusty roads

and notch off each hour
on koumboloia and squint

at the tomato trucks,
hoping that something will fly

off the top with untorn skin,
its juices held safe

from the dirty street.

DREAMING

He began with a smile like papou's.
Light moved in and out like cars
on a highway. In his tapestried room

he'd open his arms and invite me to tea,
the serving tray already set. Inside his atelier,
shaped like the inside of a drum, I could sit anywhere.

His tapestries hung around the room. Bolts of fabric leaned
against the walls. His current experiment was silver:
his satin tie, the stitching on the tapestries, the tea tray,

the streaks in his hair. The shine
from the silver merged with the light
through the window. He lived

inside a hollowed drum, inside the moments
before the summer's haze bleached out the room
and his hair, leaving only the lie of morning's light.

EL FORTUNA

for my grandmother

Not a quarter in your left hand, nor any Saturday
standing in front of the fortune-telling machine.

Not a poultice of warm spices soaking
in the bath tub. And not a medallion

etched with twigs and crows' feet. I was still
born the girl with the inward curve above my lip,

eggshells lacing the edges of my fingers, a steady
force toward uncertainty. And you are still

folded in a hospital bed, your mouth opened
like an over-ripe quince, and eyes searching

for the nurse who dabs your ears
with fresh perfume. No luck, no prayers,

no lit candles on your feast day. Not even
if I pour salts over your dearest forehead.

Not even if I roll a handful of peas
inside a sieve can I change this course.

LATE NIGHT PRAYER

Steady me inside this highway
hail-storm. Unfurl your great arm

and give me safe passage.
This night will not

even bring a forgiving thunder.
Change my course

into the smoothness
of a Florida spring,

its waters cool and free.
Untangle me from

the knotted rope,
my knuckles whitened,

my palms great with rash.
Give me a cooling crystal

to see me through this
anxious fever. And yet—

grant me strong arms,
a warm still

echoing in my ears.

WIDOW

Her arms are rivers in waiting.
She rubs roofs, mistakes torches for icicles,

surrounds her house with water. From inside her till,
she prays in sharp fragments, throws glass,

scatters along the stairs. Her life has become
something faint studded with autumn quills

and hummed memorials. All that's left
is to be set in darkening cement.

She wants to be frozen in waves
or to be like the man who breathes fire—

always proclaimed a local wonder. Ice,
of course, is melting. Everything is breaking.

FUNERAL SONG

O crooked plough, you have forgotten the disk harrow.
The years of melting and weaponry. The always-raised surface
of your mouth, even in the middle of a great dust. How
I can trace my fingers across you. What will happen now?

The field behind my old house is now full of houses.
You have been left to rust in the shackled barn,
an overgrown corner, that space beyond
the farmers' graves. How will your work song get sung?

Who will join your chorus? On visits home,
I walk by your weathered cage. For you, I will
remember the prayers for a healthy crop, the eroded
sediment, the river soil, the field of bent wheat.

INHERITANCE

Leave, hills, the unrolled sky, the clouds
like horse tails in quickening steeds. Leave

to July the thrust of dark and pavement, the low-
voiced bass like a spirit guide to the jugular. And me?

For me, the neighborhood of our evening walk,
the sticky smell of grass tripping and heady

with a great heat. O architect of my famous garret,
o arc of spiders, this is all I want.

Your silken scarf tethering my wrists, a rusty truck
with brakes old and weak like a wake-up call

too close to my kitchen window. An endless blue
and spinnerets that shoot every uninhabited space.

Someday, I can weave a cloth of this. I can make
the ways you loved me last beyond a quiet care,

the heirloom pearls still in your still ears.

ALMOST

Who knows what your stars would bode, what marled
and astral flight would be waiting, what darkening
would take root? The tubes and wires, their colors tangled

and running down your hospital bed, that expiring lot
of dye. Your bruises and veins chart their telling path.
A gag of dry rashes. Outside, patches of black ice

and a thickening cold. Daggers frozen mid-air
and waiting to mark the space for a gale wind. The things
you never knew to stitch together. A limit, another agitation,

a chart whose language needs divining. These things
you never knew to bring together, all that
I cannot read from the wrinkles in your hospital gown.

AS IF BY DREAM

New York, 1996

I am growing unsure of my heart and the world around me.
O disobedient starling, unable to control your own secretions.

O oil beetle, your after-trail slick down my throat,
your death tap a language of a different light.

One great and electric shock. Soon enough I will unravel
to little more than a face after the brightness has taken

its leave, a tilting down to your unearthly stare.
No map, no historical tract can trace these things.

Just a shoot-forth, hazy thought. And in what belief
will I find my safety? How can I veil myself?

ENDOSKELETON IN AMBER

Threat looms like the bite
of a varying hare. What is there to know
about the way I have remixed hope into something
that resembles my own inconsolable
and yellow-toothed winter?

There is little beyond that emptying estuary,
an audience unkempt and readied
in its seasonal blaze, a downward kneel
of spiders dizzy with gold.

What is left is my famous doubt.
I would like to say that I have escaped
with more than a skull to spare, lucid
at a moment's notice, an unfathomable
and fresh dress,

its bottom flare hemmed with an antique lace.
But I don't have such riches at hand, only
grandmother's damasks and a skirt scrubbed
with milk soap to fold in a rosewood chest.
I promise, instead, to be resinous,
to spin what is acidic.

JUST A PHASE

At six years old I stripped my playing dolls
of their only clothes & kept their bodies on display

along the stairway. Passers-by
closed their eyes & asked their gods for help.

At ten I washed my mother's needles, wrapped them
with thread, & hid them with the good linens.

When I was twelve I liked to lick the knives that laid
inside the kitchen drawers. No one saw.

I held my thumb to my tongue to feel
what the knives left behind.

EVERYTHING SET TO THIS WIND

                              strikes and leans
against light. Each time I question that swelled elsewhere—
a low town touching upon someone else's woods—it lies
              fixed and founded by straight-backed stars.

My city—wing-bone and stone. Swiftly washed over,
tepid and glinting,
                        scraps left behind
from the gold rush. This whole place, five counts
of restlessness and teetering architecture. Too much
to be blown away or passed over my softest beseech.

I want the inattentive glimpse and go of my eyes
to shift into an accurate trance, the force that switches
lights off at the end of day.
                              All of the fear
I wanted dead. I want to be poised and readied,
              to be sent flying.

MOVING

(While in classical myth Minos is the noble king of Crete, in Dante's
Inferno, *Minos is the demonic creature who, in Canto V, assigns*
ill-begotten souls a level in Hell in which to take new residence)

Dearest Mother,

Minos only considers the highest bidder.
Everyone grovels, lays their palms on his feet,
while he pumps his thumbs for the wealthiest and barters

in salted cashews, crimson saris, and Turkish gold. I push
through the crowd and offer my own pockets: slivers
from Zakinthos, peppermints, Matthew's phone number.

Approaching the podium is like swimming
through rubber tires: impossible. Minos may not accept
my gifts anyway. He may take his long nails

and slash the ticking of my pockets. What would I do?
I am wondering this from beneath the gnarled oak,
mangled and arthritic, *Daddy, please come home*

scratched into a limb by a child whose father
left at Minos's whim for the roasting beach,
leaving a trail of salted nuts.

I will send my address soon. Write.

Your loving S.

THE DIVINER OF STRANGE OBJECTS

Not corn barrels. Not highways. Not even
an easyfield gaze upwards, and a hope

that thin curls of sky would suggest an answer.
Instead, a false alarm when a chin song

would do. I am left with only my thin prayer
asking for even a deflated rescue plan.

Who can I ask to help me surface
this heart in four hardfield steps?

MEMOIR

Deep into thicket, a brilliant wash of jewels. A great bevel-edged
everywhere that's left after the window-maker's hands

have been scoured. And I mumble my search for my wildest edge,
the approximate center of a heart made as if more tender

in your ever-sharp after. This is the huge spirit I can't harness.
The luminous night of throats purring in unison. I think

you have become a caramel ocean, your skin a strange
softing as I travel, a pilgrim, weary and persistent,

spinning against my own hope for respite. Certain that soon enough, an oasis
will swift into vision. Certain that it will be the closest thing

to pressing myself to light. My eye speaks its own language, a garbled
rash of *soon, tornado season* and *there is a world,*

it has chased me down. I am asking you to rub an aloe and calm
this chafe. Maybe deliver me a treatise of mercy, its pages

clasped to my cellar door. I will try to conjure even the most myopic
patience, its blurred edge like a green light to welcome you with.

GHAZAL

A garden statue stands in constant meditation,
its eyes cast down in constant meditation.

In the village, a thief runs from house to house
with shortening breath. His haste, a hesitant meditation.

Inside old houses, ghosts drift
through rooms in haunting meditation.

The baker rises before dawn. He spends hours
kneading dough in diligent meditation.

Will you accept my gifts—a spoon, laughter, hyacinth stems—
as a proper trade for this dilettante's meditation?

I am sitting, Beloved, before your door.
Every day waiting, in vigilant meditation.

TATTOO

An arm winds back
into a red octopus, a Samaritan's cap.
Lanterns like glow-paper race my spine

to the bare-legged fireman,
my wooden house, outgrown flames
that scroll my direction.

Without you, my bones burn
like slick ropes. My eyes dry
and crack until all that remains

is a heavy cloud, an empty space
for you to pass on the street
as your fingers fray

into five thousand strands
and tangle in the pressing heat.
I'm striking matches.

WE CALL IT BLOSSOMING—

Blood blister inside a heel or a flaw overflowing
its heart in the heart of a troubling moment. Something
muddied, silted, beyond easy clarification.

I search for you in this space, roped away and troubled.
If in the thick of a hard winter, you—. And if,

grafting in a dark room, a squared and wooly anxiety—.
I am as if drowsy and too stupid
to find. A smaller version of you stands

off-center, feeds the pigeons near the lamp post and hopes
for an end to your own great terror: this jag of thorns

in my mouth a disappointment, a blockade along
the sidewalk of your evening walk. And in me, a doubt
crying *fracture, fracture!* in the middle of this buzzing light.

FERTILE

Somewhere after the houses burning from
beneath their heaviest frames, after

the red that rises in the wake of a recessed heat.
Somewhere after the third time

you told me to find my own hell
because I am too small to enter yours.

I am searching for the things that a younger you
begged me to depend on.

The implement to help me throw open every sallow curtain.
The issue of daybreak is important;

I am looking for what has left me here,
the something more

or less that rides out beyond
the tumbled light,

the color of river water after
the stones have been rinsed.

WHAT COMES AFTER INSUFFICIENCY

And how to account for this tectonic shift?
Somewhere, a deformational history.

Somewhere else, a careful move in the face
of strain and rift. A sort of strike

and dip to find a fair lineation
of things knotted beneath mineral veins.

Instead, an outcropping suture. Even
the rough edges of our irritable faults.

EURIPUS PHENOMENON

       This is midnight hedged in Christ's Thorn,
my feet curled deep in sand and the discotheque
burning up behind me. This wild of glass

       and drums sweating with the tide
is just another Aegean fluke trying
to convince me that night doesn't spin

       its cocoon against my stiffening back.
Tonight, it seems this world could end
at Evia. I am too far from safety boats.

       Beyond this dark,
the tidal mouth. This is the nothing
that reaches out to me.

SMALL-FACED MOMENT

Difficult enough to fasten myself
to the economy of a darkened room,

its great shudder and hardened mass
of—what? Sea salt, a ruffled slip of wrist,

the endless rash? This could be murderous,
a wall lined with shadow-girls, the hard-

knocked thought that undertow
can be found somewhere east

of a moving ship. Curved
around a sallow tug, this private loss

has nothing to do with the steel frame
too heavy to hold, the bridge

you hoped would keep shape
over my sloping sediment.

TRY SURPRISING ME

                              with a clipped newspaper
article about the latest dog show and maybe

a snapshot of the champion's owner,
a middle-aged woman with thick glasses

and meticulous hair, an unpolitical
pants suit, and an exhausted

smile. I could press this flat
between books for years and years.

When you are far away, the paper's edges
will help me imagine an older you with yellowing teeth

and a once-flattering smile turned dry and cracked
from those January nights I closed

my door and turned off my light
before your workday ended.

WHEN I MISS HIM

He is sixteen below and separated from
the sky by swamp after swamp
and miles of limestone. He has stopped

finding time to love me.
Instead, he sells radiators to anyone
who could possibly care. He lives on a bridge
tossing playing cards one by one.

In solitaire, the red and black cards
are given order. I'm shuffling the pack,
opening another game.

Everything else is buried and loose
in time like long division or an old watch
lost in a clunky safe.

THE LITTLE EPIC I'LL SING FOR YOU

Try this. A comet with a blistering tail. Its dance a splash of something
like an alley-flare. A roundabout point, a delay of its own heat,

a troubling in the late-night wild. Something to be found exactly
in the Rhodes-sky. Soft and marshed-out, you followed

the blaze just enough to unmoor and unshelter. You wanted
pity. Try this. The woman next to you fevers vibration,

and in her throat one stretch of nerve. A scattering in your ear
will become an unwelcome memory. A communal note

at the end of a long row. Your own little rage that goes unheard.
Or, instead, the last of your supplies exhausted, and you,

left at the edge of yourself. You stand crumbling and jagged
in a tense heat. You are searching for a lark song

that simply won't work. You have kept yourself dark to night's
settling in. How the sky sings its own constellational devotion.

You raise your arms as if to say, *I know how to make*
a wild resignation. I know how to crush larkspur

and brew a ruinous tea. But that's just it: you're the top
half of Orion with rain clouds veiling the belted glory.

BEFORE SIRIUS ANNOUNCES THE START OF MORNING

Who really knows what summer constellation
rises beyond my bedroom, what takes me back

to an overcast attempt at twilight, high tide
glinting with broken glass, a poplin nightshirt

and bare feet? No one's saying, though a black Sorraia
rushes me within five breaths of a burst lung.

My hair mottled, my mouth dry. The burn
that rises to my forehead. The not knowing if he

would try to tame me, the not caring that I had risen

with fever. All I know is that there was no dramatic
music, no crescendo. Not even a steady climb.

FOCUS

Light threads through
an elliptical mirror
angled towards you. Finds

its way past the unmixed fire
you dreamed into a space
that rings true enough

around my only fixed point.
Someday, like the space
between our curved surfaces,

I will be left without even
an optical tool to help me
find my way to your vacant slope.

ALABASTER

The sky is like the kids' dance,
uneven and heavy, and the snow

like their confetti, tossed
without skill. There are

no good movies and a string of nights
too cold to do much else.

I have fallen into this headwind
and landed square in a dirty snow,

my eyes witness to the unholy cold
of another January. My apartment

rings somber and empty, my body locked
into uncertain hibernation.

The tree beyond my bedroom
knocks its graying arms,

begs to come inside.

LIMIT THEORY

Instead of the space close to you at the end of the day,
this comfortable chair of sorrow and its thin, long blooms
that open after a month of hard rain. Or the water stains

in the cover of a book left too long in a basement box,
its owner unaware of the inscription you could have left

on the day you placed it in her hands. The words *relative,*
approximate of you, the price of a love, etched like the shape
of your ear's lowest curve, its break of flesh against a fresh

red wall. Like a remarkable birthmark. An etched everywhere
that begs to understand the terms of your fragile reality.

*

What if x: the weight of you when caught in a January storm
too far away to reach the bus stop. What if a binary:

I approach from an opposite distance. What if this time
the integer of you falls outside of my correct answer.

Its rules of halving and squaring: divine hope
when all other signs of you are invisible. What if

a white space: more important than the equation that interrupts.
Then maybe its own equation: luminous and blinking:

blanketing the mapped thought of what could be possible.
A shared moment across a table. The two equal things

of our coffee mugs steaming towards an indefinite sky.

ON FORGIVENESS

Everything is beholden
to a soggier district,

my smaller home of regret
and roped-off space.

The neck that bleeds
your growl and slack.

The wind won't disguise
your laugh, our obscene tangle,

all that stings
the tip of my chin.

I am left with this undertow.
My shirt,

stained with hard water,
the end of winter.

FLUSH, WITH DOLL'S EYE

After Liam Rector

Against the flat of an Amish night. My low-ground too hard
to absorb the burnt ammonia that presses my window against.

Too armed against white noise aching the air. I am set against
a till of yellow that's been set against.
                                 And I am milk-toothed,

and filled against my brim. In this, I am not even lean-to. But searching
for a single note in the chemical middle: a medicine. A slithering against.

My own approximate proof of intercession. Listless and against.
I am alight against my fear of you. Star anise against a woolen voice,

and locked in a mandolin case. A slippery parse to tell me that tonight,
the space against my feet will become clover water.
                                         That I will stay here,

as if too tacky and perfect to be up against.
                                  As if too steady
for even a demonic spin to rip apart.

STOPPED IN MY TRACKS

A tarnished slip of stars   in my pocket   and a wind

     working the edge of my coat.   Or an off-beat go of things,

another protest song.   I hope for this   instead of a

ghost of snake skin   the broken and looking   raccoon eyes

or anything else to   mark the years.

         This time

I am not so   lucky. It's a bag with a hole.   A nubby sock.

     A clear shrugged   shoulder   when my questions

grow hyperbolic: *is there a love*   *that*   *is enough?*   *Will Orion*

     ever   *return*   *to the wintering*   *beyond*   *my window?*

GREECE

Because it is too hot, I wonder instead
what it would be to tether my wrists
to the diver, to be dragged along

for the ride, to be left in a sandy bed, to be tangled
in the crazy resolve of discarded nets
and weathered boats. I wonder what it would take
for night to come. This is how I hope to die.

I want nothing of the heavy look inside my grandmother's eye
when she grasps for the smallest word, repeats it
like a trained bird, and shuffles her hands

because she is too tired to wring them right.
Or when her eyes go wide and the nurses part
her lips, insert fresh tubes. I want nothing of those

days spent walking down the street and that salty taste
rubbed along my lips. I am tracing my wrists, looking

for a rope. I am asking the man
anchoring his boat to help me.

GEOMANCY

Not a bronzed sword, nor an up-turned tea cup. Not
a drowsing chain or a winding crease, but fragments

like a sharded bottle in my carpet. Or my phone
that rings with urgency on Sunday afternoons.

Each lesson you have taught me comes small
and protruding: watch for the stray cats, the diseases

they carry. Wrap your hand around
a drenched breath. Maybe a scattering earth,

a sneezing fit. It's like this, a widened
walkway, the quiet wizening.

MARKS, MEYERS, MATTHEWSON

(headstones in the funeral yard)

Something here has gone beyond the lunar.
A slackening mouth means another black outfit,

another day left a gloomy mess and reading
the names on the graves until I reach

the Greek section. This, the place
with space still left for sale and a handful

of headstones still spelled
with their old alphabet.

But, now, a divine shut-down edging
a grave digger's plot. A re-shaping

of the pituitary gland into its own body,
a laser-brushed moment that's a simple practice

for the things that move in their slow radians.
A kind of formula I can recognize

only when you turn to me, your voice
high-pitched and dry, your eyes squinting

and pointed, a moon turning retrograde.

AUTUMN

She is dancing in her bridal gown.
Lace falls around her heels.
   The clarino sighs.
She dances alone. The whispering
leaves change colors. The same
   thing always happens.
She dances in her bridal gown.
The lace slips to the floor.
   Her dark hair tumbles
   like September's leaves
falling to the ground.

AT THE EDGE OF FAITH, ALL STORIES SEEM DEAD AND WONDERFUL

Even the ones about the cold-tongued nuns.
Even the inner circle that has lost its proper evidence.

A mother cowers in the middle
of her own distance. Somewhere, a schoolgirl
drowns. Her father crouches at the edge

of the lake, mends from his chair
at the dry goods store, wonders what it would be
to go off duty from this kind of pain.

It seems that nothing can be done. It seems
there are no more gentle words.

Darkness needles its way through a fading image
to the room I have prepared, its smooth sheets,
my invitation to where the people meet.

SELF-PORTRAIT WITH BIG STAR

To think yourself nothing more than a sub-floor, warped after the river
floods over. Maybe unusable. Maybe beyond damage. To fray

and unravel, even when your heart whispers, persistent and clear,
there is no danger. To unravel again. To hold river rocks

and wonder if they can really tell you for certain. To see yourself
as a stretch of highway. A paved and enormous arm

that stretches to its safe space. To wonder beyond what place your worth
extends. What paint falls in thin sheets from the ceiling. To write yourself

in twenty pages. The sheets of paper in front of you transposed
as the night sky, slowly falling into its late-night black. To claim

that everything framed in your windshield as you pass through Callaway
County is nothing more than a majestic force of faith and light projected

from a great distance. To start to know that there is no way to know.
But to know that it began as a collapsing cloud, the helium like fingers

lacing through hydrogen. The hold it has, just strong enough to prevent
a continued fold into itself before it decides that it is time to degenerate.

To know that all you see in your two-hour drive is the smallest pinpoint
of an old, old light. To ask yourself, *is this enough?*

A SORT OF MEMORIAL

From the edge of Turkey Creek, a cross that anyone
could make: spindles tugged from the back of a kitchen chair,
roped together, firmed in the ground with a fabric flower.
A picture of the girl who drowned. Not quite the road

from Thessaloniki to Ouranoupoli, the bus nudging down
its small road, winding carefully along the cliff, the edges
marked with the sorts of things that have become every day:
a brass stand, a light keeping watch, a gathering of icons

to guide the departed down his rightful path. And this
is not to say of the Florida thicket where I thought of you
in those years before your great decline. The way you taught me
to answer the phone with a smile. The nail files you kept

in the drawer of the television table. The stained glass sparrow
you hung from the kitchen window. The light that filtered
through, each color that spilled when you would wake
and answer the tug and call of a new day.

I THINK OF YOU AS I WALK TO JAZZBAR VOGLER

Munich, 2008

The shops along the way have long since closed.
The stones on the walk barely reach their freeze.
The Isar River, a sculpted version of itself, dulls

in the January night. Everything I see follows
the lead of the nurses who prepare for another night
of wondering how deep your sleep might be, how long

it will take for you to shut down. Everything
you could still have is no longer yours—the Ohio house
with its cement driveway. The post lamp at the edge.

The dream neighborhood of post-war houses.
The kitchen counter where we rolled the dough for apple pies.
The husband who used to sing your favorite songs

in the car on a Sunday drive. A picture
of your every love and childhood dream realized.
I am half a world away from you, asleep

and at the end of your life. I see my breath,
empty and tired in the oily and dimming street
light. How much time is left to tell you, yiayia,

about this darkness and how it can dizzy a girl?
What a thunder, to listen for what I never learned.
This indelibility. The rasping lung of night.

A PAGE FROM MY DAY BOOK

These days I have so little to conquer, just a stretch
of my back, its imperfect arc, a residual comfort
and a thin line of light across the hardwood floor.
Everything else ticks on by: the creak of a crooked doorway,

a dripping faucet, the September wind that won't
leave me alone. Nothing's lackluster. Nothing's
splendid. Sometimes I can almost convince myself to stop
caring. It could be so easy, that's how I'd like it,

just a soft place to curl up and rest my eyes. But who
would want this for me, whatever joy that could be held
in a space as small as a window pane? Instead
it's like a garden full of bindweed, an expanse

of things I am meant to learn, a geometry
and web of unsettling that scratches hard
and threatens to take root. All that I have, today:
an old bench and a dusty light, a lack of shade

and a conflicting regard, a restlessness
rising and stiffening my spine. A worn out itch
that wants to keep me here. Nothing to do
but stretch, wait, unfold in a still moment.

POEM FOR A PARTICULAR SADNESS

Sometimes, a wash of moon pooling around your feet
and the simplest words etched in an old-boned glow:
how will you come to know yourself as a climb

of smoke, a ghost-like finger to guide this sad,
small cloak around your body? How can you prepare
for how this feels, the taste of a thin slip of stars

gathered into your pockets, how in the flat
night a voice will chant *weak, weak, weak*? Could you live
without that ache in your abdomen? Your only instinct

is to crawl inside the old sadness that invites you in,
the one that feels buoyant and steady even when everything
betrays you: memories you've grafted with a forest-like hope.

Small molecules that vine their way together
until they become an opulent table—full and refined,
feasts for days piled on top. The heart

that stretches out like canvas across a wood frame
until it fills with a particular brightness. A familiar ache nestles
in your ribcage. Something flickers. The instinct to fold

inside yourself, like the ball that forms when a hand
fists its way around aluminum. What glints off an edge
like a shave of light along the waves of an old, old sea.

AMULET

If a strong jaw. If a plume more blue
than a painted door in Copenhagen.
If a space inside the nest you made
edging a weather-walled mission.

If a swallow, then an imperishable star.
Jewel-toned, then paint swifted
on the walls of a lean-to. A spiral
of cherry blossoms so bright

they spell the name my grandfather
gave me. If a love poem. If a trinket
with enamel chipped away from view.
If a granary. A storage of pots

full of barley for a winter's storm.
If constant. If a chiseled symmetry.
A way to say *the being of your hour.*

TO DEFINE DILAPIDATION

You would think a failing house on cinder blocks. The porch
crooked, weed grass poking through the slats,

somewhere near the back-forest of a highway town.
You would think the owner a guy with scurvy.

But maybe that's a bruise. A purpling on the underbelly. A force
that speaks vacancy in the cavernous mother of my heart.

Even now, years after your swollen legs stilled a hospital bed.
Your unkempt lungs barely able to whisper

their simplest want for water. Even as the wheezy sounds
worked over our shared name. Oh in those minutes

before your heart collapsed, unable to hold straight
with even the simplest foundation. Oh if I could give you

some muscle, a walking path, a new patch of grass
to surround your loveliest house. Some potted tomatoes

however long past you would smell them
and proclaim *too ripe*. Oh if I could fix that day.

ERASURE

It was the track of a rhyme spun out
from a hand-weathered radiophone.
It was the world
                    you sketched on paper
that wished thinly, above

a tangle of plastic and twine.
It was the last meditation, the space
of white and smoke, after the last hope

        for a forest to emerge
from a bramble of underbrush.
And it was the moment you felt reduced,

too close to your own extreme form,
when you thought that your constant prayer—
away with these foot falls, away with all

that is packed around me—might send you
into the river of another frozenness,
floating like you have been wanting.

NOTES STITCHED SAFELY INTO THE LINING OF GRANDMOTHER'S BEST SHAWL

I know about what hangs on the other side
of fifteen. I know about the day we picked clean

that apple tree and about skin gone shriveled
from too much dirty rain. I know about midnights in July

from beneath the raspberry bushes.
I know about what we cannot repair,

about glass set to the inside of a wrist, about the hour
you threw your arms out and gave up.

I know about the whispered everything.

OLD AGE

She opens still-set doors to what's
farther out, the growl-starred dog,

the years from now when everything
will be just another case

of bad manners. This goes for the glory-
book, its careful binding exhausted under

the weight of misuse, and for the pearls
that won't shake after years

of being unthinkable. Out of nowhere,
the roads will all stop. It will be

a simple end of gravel and tar, a patch
of witch grass. Around here, it will be

a no-barriers-needed sort of thing.
And for her, just a licked finger

smoothing an eyebrow,
and pursed lips, a quick mention

that so much has already
become unnecessary.

WEST

with the sunset fishers. Pelicans
diving, wanting one last shot.
       Pass-A-Grille Island
settles despite the tide, reminds me that I have run
my car to its very edge.
            Like a dead reckoning,
charting myself for the current that might come
as the sky turns to ink and begs me to drift
into everlastingness.
          Somewhere must be
an error. How am I left so vulnerable to evening wind?
    Where is the rooting to help me steady myself?
This is not the time to get caught in fishing line,
to be pulled in a receding wave.
  It is not my turn
to wait for Sirius to make his late appearance. This is not
      my inky table to prepare.

ACKNOWLEDGMENTS

I am grateful to the editors of the journals listed below who have published poems from this collection (sometimes in other versions):

32 Poems: "Old Age"
Anti—: "Memoir"
Barn Owl Review: "Notes Stitched Safely into the Lining of My Grandmother's Best Shawl, " "To Mary Brass," "Self-Portrait with Big Star," "We call it blossoming—," "Limit Theory," "Poem for a Particular Sadness"
Bluestem Magazine: "Greece"
Boticelli Magazine: "Flush, With Doll's Eye," "La Fortuna," "Alabaster"
Columbia: A Journal of Literature and Art: "Amulet"
Contrary Magazine: "Endoskeleton in Amber"
Fifth Wednesday: "Euripus Phenomenon"
Grist: A Journal for Writers: "The Little Epic I'll Sing For You," "Slow Fail"
Harpur Palate: "Funeral Song"
Laurel Review: "Everything set to this wind," "West"
Matter: A Monthly Journal of Political Poetry and Commentary: "Inside a Dark Room"
Pebble Lake Review: "I Think of You as I Walk to Jazzbar Vogler"
Phoebe: "And in the middle of," "Marks, Meyers, Matthewson"
St. Katherine's Review: "Erasure," "What Comes after Insufficiency"
Sou'wester: "Inheritance"
Subtropics: "When I Miss Him"
Thrush Poetry Journal: "To Define Dilapidation," "As If By Dream," "Fertile," "At the Edge of Faith, All Stories Seem Dead and Wonderful"
Waccamaw: "Widow"

I am also grateful to the composer Stefanie Lubkowski, who used "Inside a Dark Room" as the lyrics to a song of the same title.

Personal thanks to the mentors, teachers, friends, and colleagues who have helped nurture these poems: Sidney Wade, Lucie Brock-Broido, Scott Cairns, Aliki Barnstone, Amy Newman, Josh Robbins, Virginia Konchan, Gary McDowell, John Nieves, Charlotte Pence, Amanda Auchter, and Sandy Longhorn. My gratitude must also be extended to the group of writers who met on Sargent Street in North Cambridge,

MA, for summertime margaritas & magic as well as my group of writers and literary critics at the University of Missouri; without both of these communities, these poems would not have come into this world.

I would be remiss if I didn't show gratitude for Ron Starbucks' editorial leadership and collaborative spirit in bringing this book to life.

Most of all, I am grateful for the support and love of my family—Anita, Stamatios, and Bill—and, above all else, Tom, who brings light into every room.

NOTES

"The Diviner of Strange Objects" owes a small debt to Sidney Wade. The line, "Instead, a false alarm when even a chin song// would do" takes inspiration from Sidney Wade's poem titled "Chin Song."

"*We call it blossoming*—" takes its title from the penultimate line of Jorie Graham's poem, "Tennessee June."

"Small-Faced Moment" owes another debt to Sidney Wade, whose poem "Weight of Light" includes the lines, "In this moment, sowing its great and murderous/ swindle overseas, the state/ efficiently removes the available light from the air/ of thousands of darkened rooms. The economy/ requires it."

ABOUT THE AUTHOR

Stephanie Kartalopoulos earned her PhD in English from the University of Missouri, where she was a Creative Writing Fellow for Poetry from 2008-2012. She lives in Atlanta, where she teaches writing and literature.

www.ingramcontent.com/pod-product-compliance
Lightning Source LLC
Chambersburg PA
CBHW080749250626
47162CB00010B/3069